Launching an
Orphans Ministry
in your church

Jason Weber
with Paul Pennington

FAMILYLIFE
Publishing™

Little Rock, Arkansas

Launching an Orphans Ministry in Your Church
© 2006 by FamilyLife.
All rights reserved. First edition 2006.

11 10 09 08 07 06 1 2 3 4 5 6 7 8 9 10

ISBN-10 1-57229-989-4
ISBN-13 978-1-57229-989-4

Printed in the United States.

Author: Jason Weber, with Paul Pennington
Editors: Tim Grissom, Amy Bradford
Proofreader: Fran Taylor
Cover design: Rob Green
Interior layout: Jerry McCall

Scripture taken from the NEW AMERICAN STANDARD BIBLE®, Copyright © 1960, 1962, 1963, 1968, 1971, 1972, 1973, 1975, 1977, 1995 by The Lockman Foundation. Used by permission.

Dennis Rainey, President
5800 Ranch Drive
Little Rock, Arkansas 72223
1-800-FL-TODAY
www.familylife.com

Contents

Eight Steps to Launching an Orphans Ministry in Your Church

Eight On-Board Tools to Help You Get Started

Appendices

Dedications

To the love of my life, Trisha, whose care for "the least of these" continues to be my example.
—Jason

To Robin, my best friend, my true companion, and one whose love for our children shines with light from heaven. And to Elizabeth, Kit, Seth, Ethan, Hope, and Noah from whom I have seen what blessing really means and from whom I have learned some of God's best lessons.
—Paul

Acknowledgments

There are a number of church orphans ministry leaders whose faith and example provide the vision for this book: that one church—any church—can be used by God to make an eternal difference in the lives of countless orphans and waiting children. Some of these instrumental church orphans ministry champions include: Suzanne Faske, Chris and Sara Padbury, Kent Hatfield, and Maridel Sandberg. A very special thanks to Michael Monroe of Irving Bible Church who has provided very valuable feedback and whose fingerprints can be found throughout this guide.

Ronnie Girouard and Pam Dunavant have been our companions each day in the Hope for Orphans department at FamilyLife. As God continues to move mightily in this area of orphan care, we continue to enjoy hanging on for dear life with you guys.

Special thanks to the FamilyLife Publishing and creative resource teams who are wonderful to work with and who have bent over backwards on this one. You are the best.

(Jason here) Thank you to everyone who has played a part in launching the orphans ministry at my home church, Mosaic Church of Central Arkansas. Much of what is in these pages was learned while walking with you.

(Paul here) I would like to thank Dennis and Barbara Rainey, for not only recognizing the invitation to join God in His work to care for orphans, but also for allowing my family to experience God's reality thru serving with the folks at FamilyLife and Hope for Orphans. I would also like to acknowledge the late Russell Kelfer of Wayside Chapel in San Antonio, Texas, our shepherd for almost 20 years, whose teaching and encouragement led to much of the early vision of Hope for Orphans.

Foreword

In the earliest years of the Christian church, followers of Christ were known as people who would put their lives and their comforts on the line for the sake of the poor, the sick, the widowed, and the orphaned. Throughout history, however, the concern for "the least of these" has fluctuated: while the Christian community has embraced the needs of orphans in some seasons, in others it has been found lacking.

Today there is a fresh movement of God's Spirit in the church to once again engage critical issues surrounding orphans. Christians are taking bold and courageous steps to act on behalf of the orphan and waiting child. Some are deciding to adopt, others are engaging in foster care, and many are making the strategic decision to mobilize their entire church to find various ways to care for orphans and waiting children. The results are very encouraging: one church mobilized its community to adopt over forty children from two orphanages in Kazakhstan. Another church is adopting and caring for over seventy children in foster care. Still another is working to bring about the adoption of almost eight hundred waiting children in its state's foster-care system. Scores of other churches are revolutionizing orphan care through their involvement in the lives of thousands of orphans and waiting children in the U.S. and around the world.

Almost all of these churches have one thing in common: their work with orphans began with the vision of one person.

Perhaps in your church, that person is you.

If so, please allow us to help. We have created this guide to provide you with the practical information you need to mobilize allies and successfully launch an orphans ministry in and through your church. In addition to providing information, we have also provided *On-Board Tools* that will help you execute each of the eight steps involved in the process of launching an orphan-care ministry in your church.

As you read this guide, I believe your vision for what God can do through your church will expand. My hope is that you will gain confidence to step out in faith on behalf of these children and, as Psalm 82:3 says, "vindicate the weak and fatherless."

At this unique time in history, God is working within His church to care for the orphan in unprecedented ways. Will you join Him in this worldwide movement? I look forward to hearing how God uses you and your church.

Dennis Rainey
President, FamilyLife
Little Rock, Arkansas

I thank God for Dennis Rainey and his team at FamilyLife. I rejoice in the growing vision for the sacred calling of adoption. The pain and pleasures of parenting are multiplied with every child we embrace—at whatever age and by whatever means. The rewards are partly in this life, but mainly in the next. Jesus does not call us to maximize our securities and comforts here. He said, "Whoever loses his life for my sake will find it." The short-term risks of adoption are huge. The long-term risks of love are zero. God will make all grace abound for every day's demand. Nothing is impossible with Him. There will be no regrets for parents who love in the power of Christ. May God multiply churches that live this truth.

—John Piper, Pastor for Vision and Preaching
Bethlehem Baptist Church

Introduction

When you reap your harvest in your field and have forgotten a sheaf in the field, you shall not go back to get it; it shall be for the alien, for the orphan, and for the widow, in order that the Lord your God may bless you in all the work of your hands.

Deuteronomy 24:19

In ancient Israel, God had expectations of what his followers should do for those who had the least. This passage in Deuteronomy demonstrates His specific expectations on behalf of the alien, the orphan, and the widow. Verses 20-22 mention leaving olives on the trees and grapes on the vines for these same three groups of people. God was asking His people to give part of their most precious commodities away so that others might live.

We believe that God still has expectations of what His followers should do for those in need. However, as C. Thomas Davis points out in *Fields of the Fatherless* it can be hard to discern what that means anymore. What does it look like in our society to leave our grain, our olives, and our grapes for others? What is God asking of us today? What are our most precious commodities?

There are many things in modern society that are precious to us. However, when it comes to caring for those who are most often forgotten, our resources of greatest value include finances and time.

American Christians are among the wealthiest on earth. Our capacity to change some of the difficult realities for the "least of these" (Matthew 25:40) is unprecedented. But perhaps more than wealth, we have more difficulty giving others our time.

Making a real life-long impact in the life of another takes time. And time, it seems, is scarce. But when we make the decision to give to the poor and the oppressed, the results are matchless:

And if you give yourself to the hungry
And satisfy the desire of the afflicted,
Then your light will rise in darkness
And your gloom will become like midday.
And the Lord will continually guide you,
And satisfy your desire in scorched places,
And give strength to your bones;
And you will be like a watered garden,
And like a spring of water whose waters do not fail.

Isaiah 58:10-11

The pages that follow represent one way that you can give yourself to the least of these. Specifically, we have attempted to give you the tools and information you need to mobilize your church to launch a ministry specifically for orphans and waiting children. We have outlined this process in eight steps and have provided tools that will give you much of what you need.

As you read, you will encounter many exciting ideas that have been implemented by churches across the country. As you encounter these ideas, you may find yourself saying, "That's great, but how do I do it?" The purpose of this guide is to provide you with the basic information you need to launch an orphans ministry. Once you have launched, you may need continued help knowing where to turn to execute the ideas God has given you. We at FamilyLife's Hope for Orphans ministry want to be a continuing resource to offer insights and suggestions and to help you make connections with the best organizations in orphan care.

For example, if you want to take a group from your church on a mission trip to an orphanage, we can point you to great organizations that are experts in that. If you want to start an adoption fund, again we know where to turn. In fact, you will find much of this type of information in Appendix B in the back of this guide.

Our prayer is that in reading this guide and implementing its steps you will come to understand what God is asking you and your church to do on behalf of the orphan, and that you would have the courage to step out in faith and do it. God wants to use you and thousands of others like you to demonstrate His love for those who are alone, showing what it means today to leave our sheaves behind.

Eight Steps

to Launching
an Orphans Ministry
in Your Church

Eight
Steps
at a Glance

STEP 1: Approach a Key Leader with Your Vision

In order to start the process, someone in a key position of leadership needs to know your intentions and have the opportunity to guide your efforts. You will need to find the right leader in your church and help them to understand both your desire to start an orphans ministry and your intentions to assemble a team of people and a plan of action.

STEP 2: Identify Passionate Families to Join You in Prayer

Likely, there are people in your church right now who would love to give their time and talents to the needs of the orphan. Your job is to identify them and then lead them to earnestly seek God's direction for their next steps.

STEP 3: Dream Together About the Possibilities

Through the process of seeking God's will and talking with your team, there will be many ideas and dreams that come to mind. Collect those ideas and prayerfully begin to determine what God has put in the heart of your team.

STEP 4: Determine Your Channels of Orphans Ministry

At this point, some ideas will have surfaced regarding the general direction your ministry will go. You will find yourself moving toward at least one of the three channels of orphans ministry, if not all three: (1) orphan care, (2) adoption—international and private domestic, and (3) foster care and foster-care adoption.

STEP 5: Plan the Strategies of Your Ministry

Look at your current situation and your long-term goals and determine the strategies that will best accomplish the objectives God has given you. These strategies can be categorized into five modes: (1) prayer, (2) physical needs, (3) financial assistance, (4) education, awareness, and recruitment, and (5) support ministry. Each of these modes can be executed in the context of the three channels discussed in step 4.

STEP 6: Establish the Proposed Leadership Structure

You have managed to accomplish several important steps. Now it is time to formalize the leadership structure of your proposed ministry and to assign specific leadership roles.

STEP 7: Develop a Formal Proposal for Church Leadership

You have the basic building blocks to assemble a good plan for your church leaders to consider. Now you need to merge everything you have developed into one cohesive and well-conceived plan that you will present to the key leaders in your church for their approval and blessing (pastoral staff, elders, deacons, board of trustees, etc.).

STEP 8: Launch Your Orphans Ministry!

The launch of your church's orphans ministry is an exciting time. Engaging the entire church at this stage is key to gaining momentum and building your ministry. Once you have launched, it is time to implement your first initiatives, work in partnership with others, and celebrate what God does.

Step 1 — Approach a key leader with your vision

Because every church is unique, knowing how to set up a new ministry can be challenging. It is important to have someone in leadership who understands your vision and who can provide feedback as you navigate through the process at your church. Your goal in approaching this person is not to get final approval on starting an orphans ministry. That comes later. For now, you are merely seeking approval to work toward building a team, constructing a plan, and presenting it to a broader representation of church leadership.

Who should this key leader be? Most likely it will be someone on the pastoral staff or one who serves as an elder or deacon. Look for two things when determining whom to approach:

1. Role—Some churches have staff assigned to various areas, any of which might be an obvious fit for orphans ministry (e.g., children's pastor, community outreach pastor, missions pastor). You want to find someone whose department has clear synergy with your vision of caring for orphans.

2. Life Experience—You may find that there is a person in a position of leadership whose area is not especially tied to orphans ministry, but because of his or her own life experiences, he or she would make an excellent liaison. This person may be an adoptive parent, have been adopted, or have spent significant time ministering in orphanages. They may already have the passion for what you are doing and are excited to help in any way they can.

Once you have identified this key leader, you will want to meet with them and cast the vision for orphans ministry. This might include telling your story as it pertains to orphans. It may also involve telling the stories of other churches that have initiated an orphans ministry and describing what God is doing through them. You will have three primary objectives in approaching this leader. Help them understand

- the importance of an orphans ministry.
- the vision you have to help your church launch an orphans ministry.
- that you are not asking *them* to start the ministry, but that you need them as an ally to give helpful feedback along the way.

Pothole Ahead

Getting It

What if you walk away from the meeting with your key leader and you say to yourself, "I just don't know if he gets it"? You may find that your church leaders don't yet have the vision and passion for this ministry that you do. Don't let this discourage you. Remember, others have passions that you don't. One of the greatest roles you have been called to—as an advocate of the orphan and waiting child—is to help people "get it." Many people who have approached church leaders about this type of ministry received neither a firm yes nor a firm no. There was simply ambivalence. Part of this may be due to the fact that church leaders are often approached by members of their congregation who are excited about getting a new program started only to see it abandoned in short order. So, if you encounter reluctance from your church leader, what should you do?

1. Pray that God will give you the wisdom to articulate the vision He has given you.
2. Pray that God would enable you to proceed in ways that demonstrate a commitment to sustained ministry.
3. Tell stories about how God has worked in other churches. Jesus relied on *stories* to help motivate. People need to see flesh and bones on a concept in order to fully appreciate its significance.
4. Talk with other church orphans ministry leaders (see Appendix C). Seek out some experienced leaders who can share with you ways that they were able to help others "get it."

On-Board Tool 1   Page 30

A Vision for Orphans Ministry DVD

On the inside of the back cover you will find a DVD that will help you cast the vision for an orphans ministry to leaders in your church. This video includes interviews with pastors and church orphans-ministry leaders from around the country. It also includes the moving story of a Colorado church that God is using in remarkable ways to make a difference for foster children in that state.

Other Tools and Ideas

Ask your leader to look at one of the following two resources:

- *The Christian's Response to the Fatherless* DVD featuring Dennis and Barbara Rainey
- *Fields of the Fatherless* by C. Thomas Davis

For these tools and many others, visit www.HopeforOrphans.com.

Ordinary People, Extraordinary Impact

by Sabrina Beasley

Aimeé and Tommy Poché struggled with infertility. But one day they felt God was calling them in a different direction to multiply their family, so they stopped the treatments they were receiving. It was then that they pursued adopting a little girl from Peru, and in the meantime they adopted a baby brother for her from their home state of Louisiana.

"We adopted both of our children within two months, and when we came back the church just embraced us," Aimeé says. It was then that their pastors approached Aimeé and Tommy about starting an orphans ministry in their church. "We had never thought about that," admits Aimeé, "but it made so much sense. We were excited."

The Pochés didn't know how to start an orphans ministry, so Aimeé started researching the topic via the Internet. There she found information about a ministry that focuses on assisting adoptive parents financially. An associate there gave Aimeé contact information for another ministry that concentrates on adoption education and developing new ministries.

They were encouraged to attend an adoption conference, and they found the information they needed during a break-out session on equipping churches to start an adoption ministry. "Whatever they said to do, we did," Aimeé says. Together Tommy and Aimeé came up with a plan, beginning with communicating their vision and educating the congregation.

They named their ministry His Heart for Orphans. And within months, they had started adoption workshops and fundraiser events providing $7,000 to adoptive families after their first trial.

"Our church emphasizes the fact that ordinary people can do extraordinary things for God," says Aimeé. "You don't have to be a pastor or a person with degrees or in Bible college; you can be a regular person that God has called to make an impact in His kingdom."

Step 2 — *Identify passionate families to join you in prayer*

Orphans ministry in the local church *must* be built on a foundation of prayer. Gathering a team of committed people to pray together is vital. There are certain people in your church who are most likely to have a passion for orphans ministry. You will want to identify a group of these "seed families" and personally challenge them to join you in seeking the Lord for what He would have your church do on behalf of the fatherless. As you look at your church, think through the following categories. In the blanks provided, write the names of those who fit in each one. (This would be good to do with your key leader from Step 1.)

Adoptive Parents _____

_____

Foster Parents _____

_____

Adult Adoptees _____

_____

Foster-Care Alumni _____

_____

Adoptive Grandparents _____

_____

Social Workers _____

_____

Lawyers and Judges in Juvenile and Family Law _____

_____

Counselors _____

_____

Physicians Specializing in Pediatrics and Special Needs _____

_____

Teachers _____

_____

Alumni of Short-Term Mission Trips to Orphanages _____

_____

It will be important for these seed families to spend time together for the purpose of developing a common understanding of the need for orphans ministry, adoption of children into godly homes, and God's heart for the orphan. Your goal as a team will be to establish a common vision of what an orphans ministry *could be* in your church. Sharing ideas and getting "on the same page" will be crucial because the seed families will be ambassadors of the orphans ministry to your church's leadership and to the members of your congregation.

It might be tempting to gather these families, pray for *only* a few minutes to begin the meeting, and then proceed with ideas and dreams. However, it is crucial to remember that your goal is not simply to do something good for orphans; your goal is to *discover God's invitation for your church* in the area of orphans ministry. This can only be done through concentrated prayer. On-Board Tool 2 provides some guidance in terms of what to pray for at this stage.

Pothole Ahead _____

The Sure Thing

You may find that some of the families you are *certain* will want to be involved are not as excited as you thought they would be. Just because someone has adopted or fits one of the other categories does not necessarily mean they currently have a vision for orphans ministry in a larger context. Don't be discouraged. Instead, "ask the Lord of the harvest to send out workers into his harvest field" (Luke 10:2) and trust that He will provide exactly whom you need to carry out His work.

On-Board Tool 2 _____ Page 31

Prayer Guide

This guide will help your group pray through some of the key issues involved in seeking God's invitation for your church.

Other Tools and Ideas_____

- Invite prospective seed couples to your home for fellowship, prayer, and discussion of the prospect of starting an orphans ministry in your church. Do a four- to six-week Bible study on God's heart for orphans. A good resource for this is the book *Fields of the Fatherless* by C. Thomas Davis.
- Consider having the seed families, as a team, attend FamilyLife's "If You Were Mine" adoption workshop. (Call 1-800-FL-TODAY or visit www.HopeforOrphans.com for more information.)
- View and discuss Dennis and Barbara Rainey's message *The Christian's Response to the Fatherless* on DVD from FamilyLife.

For these tools and many others, visit www.HopeforOrphans.com.

After you have gathered at least once or twice for prayer with the other seed families, it is time to get some ideas down on paper. As the old adage goes "no idea is a bad idea." Dream. Dream big. And whatever you dream, write it down (flip charts with adhesive strips on the back of the paper work well). Don't spend a lot of time discussing the merits of each idea. The goal is to record many ideas; you can weed through them later. The purpose of this time is not so much to develop a strategy as it is to get the seed families thinking about the possibilities.

Once you have recorded your ideas, give each person five "points" (sticker dots are excellent for this). Have each person place their points by the ideas they are most excited about. If they want, they can use all five for one idea. At the end of this exercise, you will have a clearer sense of how God has wired your particular group for orphans ministry. Knowing this will make the next step much easier.

On-Board Tool 3 _____ Page 33

Brainstorming Discussion Starter

This tool will help your group to begin "thinking big" about how God might want to use your church.

Other Tools and Ideas_____

Before your brainstorming session, assign each person to contact one orphan-care organization and/or church orphans ministry (listed in Appendices B and C) to ask about potential ideas for your church. This will prove to be very helpful.

Watch the On-Board Tool 1 as a group. This DVD may spark some thoughts about potential ideas for your orphans ministry.

Small Town, Big Dreams

by Sabrina Beasley

Babies were abandoned in a room and left there to die. When Jay and Suzanne Faske were engaged, they were moved by a documentary film that highlighted how orphans in other parts of the world were treated. They also saw that the orphanages overflowed with frail-bodied children. It was then, before they were even married, that the Faskes decided they would one day adopt children of their own.

Now, after adopting several children, Jay and Suzanne started Forever Families, an adoption support ministry in their church, First Baptist of Brenham, Texas. "As the mother of adopted kids, I was always getting invitations to events for kids from India or Russia," says Suzanne, "but I had never been invited to a Christian support group for adoptive parents that included all nationalities."

With a burden on her heart and a plan in mind, Suzanne met with the mission board. She wanted to start an adoption support group. The church backed the idea wholeheartedly, but Suzanne and Jay were left to start the group on their own. "It was overwhelming at first," Suzanne says, "but we just began by focusing on awareness. And then it just kind of went from there."

At first Suzanne used just a church bulletin board to display information and pictures of waiting children to make the congregation aware of the needs of orphans. Soon, she started Christian support groups for families with adopted children in the community, and the new ministry grew so rapidly that they outgrew their facilities.

Even though the support groups of Forever Families were going well, God's work had only just begun. Suzanne's greatest desire was to see children adopted. She went to the elder board of her church to propose a "hosting" program, in which children from orphanages in Kazakhstan would be brought to the United States to live with families for a month. This would give each child the opportunity to experience being a part of a family, and the family an opportunity to consider adopting that child.

Some in the church gave money, some gave clothes, some hosted. Regardless, members made the necessary sacrifices to bring twenty-nine children from Kazakhstan for the summer, with the intention of finding them permanent homes. In the end, some couples decided to adopt more, and [forty-one] Kazak children found homes in Texas.

This ministry has already grown far beyond Suzanne's expectations. "If [forty-one] children could get families in a small Texas town," says Suzanne, "think about what other churches could do."

Determine your channels of orphans ministry

When one thinks about ministry to orphans and waiting children, several images come to mind. For some, the concept of orphans ministry equals adoption. Others envision trips to other parts of the world, taking clothing and supplies to children who may never be adopted. Whatever comes to your mind when thinking about orphans ministry, it most likely falls into one of three categories or *channels*. Each of these channels can be lived out in hundreds of ways. One helpful way to sort through the possibilities you imagined in the previous step is to determine which of these channels your ministry would like to pursue. Some choose to focus entirely on one channel while others might engage all three. Here are the definitions of each:

Channel 1: Orphan Care

In the orphan-care channel, your goal is to provide for the physical, emotional, and spiritual needs of orphans and waiting children.

Channel 2: International and Private Domestic Adoption

In this channel, your church will set up a ministry designed to educate, encourage, and support families as they consider and pursue international or domestic adoption.

Channel 3: Foster Care and Foster-Care Adoption

The United States foster-care system involves some unique needs that a specialized church ministry can address in some powerful ways. This can include ministering to state child-welfare workers, raising up and supporting foster parents, recruiting and supporting adoptive parents for children in foster care, and much more.

One of the most important things you can do at this stage is to make sure you understand what is going on in other areas of the church that might relate to orphans ministry. For example, some churches have a missions strategy that focuses entirely on one country. In this case it would make sense to consider building your orphans ministry with an emphasis in that country. Another example might be that your community outreach pastor has developed a mentorship program for at-risk children. It would then be worth considering working with that program to develop a component for foster children. This kind of deliberate coordination will not only make your ministry more effective, it will help you avoid possible tensions with other ministries where overlap is perceived.

Pothole Ahead

What's in a Name?

Choosing a name for your new ministry seems fairly straightforward, right? Well, maybe not. Consider some implications when choosing how you will refer to your ministry.

1. **Use of the word "orphan" or "orphans ministry"**
   The word "orphan" has fallen out of fashion to some extent, especially in professional child welfare circles. Part of this has to do with the fact that many children commonly referred to as orphans are not orphans in the strict sense of the term. For example, children may be in foster care because of abuse or neglect, or they may be in an orphanage due to the extreme poverty of their family. In both cases, all biological parents may still be alive. If you choose to pursue the foster-care channel, you may want to consider not referring to your ministry as an orphans ministry exclusively and thus raise the objections of the professionals with whom you are trying to build bridges. One church that focuses on all three channels states that they are their church's "ministry to orphans and waiting children." However, it should be noted that, biblically, the word *orphan* was applied to children who lost either one or both parents.

2. **Adoption ministry**
   Calling yourselves an "adoption ministry" has its advantages, especially if you are focusing primarily on Channel 2. However, consider that certain members of leadership might falsely perceive this as a ministry for only a very small number of couples and, therefore, be less significant than ministries that address larger portions of the church. A second consideration is that some church leaders have taken issue with the term "adoption ministry" because they don't want to signal that the church is engaging in adoption placement as a licensed adoption entity.

These issues need not eliminate any options for naming your church's ministry. They should simply serve as springboards for discussion among your group of seed families and with church leadership.

Current Situation Evaluation

This tool will help your team assess how God may have already equipped your church for significant orphans ministry in certain channels.

Other Tools and Ideas_____

Ask members of your seed family group to investigate one of the following areas, according to their interests, and report back to the group:

- existing ministries in the church with whom there might be synergy

- the orphan-care channel

- the international and private domestic adoption channel

- the foster care and foster-care adoption channel

At this time it would be beneficial to identify the person in your group of seed families who has some experience with strategic planning to help facilitate the next couple of steps. There are many methods for strategic planning; however, the key is to begin with the end in mind. Always keep in view what your ultimate goals are. There can be a tendency at this stage to become so immersed in strategies and tactics that the commitment to prayer loses priority. Continually seek God's direction throughout the process.

Orphans-ministry strategies can be categorized into five modes. They are:

Mode 1: Prayer

Mode 2: Physical Needs

Mode 3: Financial Assistance

Mode 4: Education, Awareness, and Recruitment

Mode 5: Support Ministry

The strategy chart on the following pages gives examples of how each of these modes can be lived out for each of the three channels from the previous step.

	Mode 1 Prayer	Mode 2 Physical Needs
Channel 1 **Orphan Care**	Select an orphanage and enlist families in your church to pray for each child on a regular basis. Maintain contact with the orphanage for updated prayer requests.	Organize a drive at your church to gather resources such as shoes, toiletries, or school supplies for orphanages. There are several organizations that can provide everything you need to organize such a drive (see Appendix B).
Channel 2 **International and Private Domestic Adoption**	Partner with an adoption agency that has a special needs adoption program. Post pictures of waiting children on a bulletin board and ask your congregation to pray that these children would be adopted.	Establish a ministry in your church that throws a shower for every child adopted by one of your church members.
Channel 3 **Foster Care and Foster-Care Adoption**	Build a relationship with a local foster-care office and regularly ask for prayer requests from the social workers there. Commit as a church to pray for these workers and the children they serve.	Partner with your local foster-care office to host a back-to-school party for the foster children in your city and their foster families. Provide each child with a backpack and school supplies.

Mode 3 Financial Assistance	Mode 4 Education, Awareness, and Recruitment	Mode 5 Support Ministry
Mobilize your church to conduct a child sponsorship drive. For four to six weeks, see how many families in your church would be willing to sponsor a child on a monthly basis.	Work with your pastor to organize an Orphans Sunday. The subject of caring for orphans could be incorporated into all aspects of the service. This could include the message, a video presentation of an orphanage mission trip, and having orphan-care organizations set up displays in the church lobby.	Your congregation can sponsor an orphanage long-term. This sponsorship can include ongoing financial support, sending teams to make improvements, deliver supplies, conduct Vacation Bible Schools, and much more The children in your church can also establish a letter-writing ministry to your sponsored orphanage.
Establish an adoption financial assistance fund through your church. There are some great organizations that can walk you through this process (see Appendix B).	Host an adoption expo that would include displays by area agencies, testimonies by adoptive families, and instruction about the adoption process.	Establish an adoption support group that meets on a regular basis. These times can be as structured or as unstructured as the group would like to make them.
Establish a fund to help meet the spontaneous needs of foster parents in your church. Often, foster families receive children of various ages with no advance notice. This emergency fund could be used to buy anything from car seats for young children to bedroom furniture for teenagers.	Enlist local professional photographers and framers to donate their services to producing photographs of waiting children in foster care. Coordinate a photo gallery (often known as a Heart Gallery) in a high traffic area of your church. For greater reach, make it a traveling gallery and invite other area churches to host the gallery in their facility for one month at a time.	Offer your facilities and qualified members of your congregation to your local foster-care office to serve as facilitators for foster-child support groups. This is often a very real need and a great way for your church to serve the community.

Pothole Ahead – Two of them!

The Either/Or Syndrome

People tend to be passionate about the things they have experienced. If you have chosen to pursue more than one orphans-ministry channel, don't be surprised when, for example, a couple in your group that has adopted from foster care and a couple that has adopted from, say, Korea have different ideas about which initiatives should be a priority. This reality has been known to cause some degree of tension in budding church orphans ministries. For some it becomes an issue of magnitude vs. proximity. The international camp feels that because there are so many more children overseas, this should be the priority. The foster-care camp often feels that those children who are closer, "in our own backyard," should be tended to first. Help those in your group to understand that wherever there are children without families, they are a priority. The key is to proceed with Philippians 2:3-4 in mind:

> *Do nothing from selfishness or empty conceit, but with humility of mind regard one another as more important than yourselves; do not merely look out for your own personal interests, but also for the interests of others.*

Guilt by Association

If you have chosen to make international and domestic adoption one of your orphans-ministry channels, some might suggest that your church develop a somewhat exclusive partnership with an adoption agency you trust. However, we strongly discourage you from doing so. What can happen (and has happened to others) is that your ministry will become associated with that agency in the minds of the people in your church. If any of them have difficulty with that agency, your ministry will be perceived to be partially at fault not only by the involved families but also by church leadership. This has caused difficulties in some churches.

This can get especially touchy if one of your seed families either owns or works at an agency and is suggesting this kind of partnership. Our recommendation is that you politely decline any exclusive or semi-exclusive partnerships with an agency and instead find three to five agencies you feel comfortable with. In any materials you give to your congregation about these agencies, be *clear* that the responsibility to fully investigate any agency is theirs and that they will need to exercise due diligence in asking questions and checking references.

Strategy Development Worksheet

This tool is designed to help your team think about what strategies will best help you to accomplish your end goals in orphans ministries.

Other Tools and Ideas

Ask two or three existing church orphans ministries (see Appendix C) about their long-term goals and the steps they are taking to get there.

From Adoption to Ministry

by Jennifer Abegg

Rod and Sonja Elofson became concerned about the welfare of parentless children and infants around the world. Rod and Sonja originally planned to adopt some children from India, but that adoption fell through. During that process, however, they were startled to learn that thousands of orphans, even babies, in their own country—America—never get a place to call home, never get a mom and dad.

These children, simply because of the color of their skin, are tossed from home to home and never receive permanent parents.

When Rod and Sonja discovered this, they applied to adopt an African-American infant. Almost immediately, they received a phone call about a baby boy who needed a home. They named their new son Micah. Soon they adopted a daughter, Kara.

When friends of the Elofsons and others realized that all these minority children needed homes, they were willing to adopt. But then after finding out the cost—about $10,000—some realized that they couldn't afford it.

That's how the MICAH fund was started. Named after the Elofsons fourth child and first adoptee, MICAH also stands for Minority Infant Child Adoption Help. It's an outreach of Bethlehem Baptist Church in Minneapolis, Minnesota, that began in 1989. Using donations from other Christians who want to be used in orphan ministry, the MICAH fund helps Christians pay for the costs so that orphans could be placed in the homes of Christ-followers.

Bruce and Maridel Sandberg were the recipients of some of that assistance. In the early 1990s, they had three children and Maridel wanted more. They heard about African-American babies that needed homes. So they decided to adopt. MICAH required that they go through a home study from an approved agency and an interview, and then the people on the committee would determine the need.

With the help of MICAH, the Sandbergs brought home Joshua. "My husband was afraid that he would not love Joshua as much as he loved our biological son," says Maridel. "But the act of adopting gave Bruce a clear picture of the gospel. It touched Bruce personally. He fell head-over-heels in love right away."

In no time, they wanted to adopt again. Then again and again and again. They have added five minority children to their family. "I call them my children of destiny," says Maridel. "God had a purpose and plan that could not be accomplished if they stayed in their birthmothers' arms—like Moses." Now she and Bruce sit on the MICAH board. "It's bigger than adoption, it's a ministry to orphans," says Maridel. Since its inception, the MICAH fund has helped place more than 225 children in Christian homes.

Step 6 — Establish a leadership structure

Once you have determined some initial strategies you would like to implement, it is time to establish a leadership structure so that these strategies can be effectively executed. Allowing the orphans ministry to run under the leadership of the seed families for too long can be a problem. These families are passionate about the cause, but they may not be able to make the commitment to ongoing planning and implementation. As a result, your meetings may begin to have different sets of people at each one, which makes it difficult to maintain continuity and to move forward.

By establishing a leadership structure you are accomplishing some key goals:

1. Streamlining the decision-making process

2. Identifying those with the ability and desire to handle ongoing strategy and administration

3. Demonstrating to church leadership that you are committed to the effective implementation of this ministry

Your church may have a suggested or even required leadership structure for new ministries. For example, we're aware of a church that requires that every new ministry have at least three people on its leadership team. The idea is that one person would focus on vision and team facilitation, the second would focus on communication with the congregation and church leadership, and the third would focus on administrative matters, including financial issues and documentation.

If your church does not have a prescribed structure, it would be a good idea to consider what you perceive to be the best-run ministries in your church. Meet with their leaders and ask how their structure has been established. Then create a document that clearly outlines the roles of each position on the leadership team.

As you flesh out your leadership team, you may find that some of your seed families have no desire to be involved in strategy development or leadership. They simply want to take a strategy that has been determined and run with it. They don't like strategy meetings—they want to DO something. These are vital people to have involved with your ministry, but they may not express an interest in the *leadership team*.

Pothole Ahead

The Lone Ranger

There have been instances of ministries that have managed to survive with one person bearing the weight of the leadership responsibility. However, as a general rule, this is not recommended. For the growth and long-term sustainability of a ministry, it is best to have a group of at least three committed leaders. This allows you to have a group of like-minded people holding one another up and dividing the workload.

On-Board Tool 6 _____ Page 40

Leadership Structure Worksheet

This tool will help you think through the key issues involved in determining how the leadership of your orphans ministry will be structured.

Other Tools and Ideas

Call other local churches that have successful ministries and interview the ministry leader about their leadership structure.

If your church doesn't have a recommended structure, ask seed families to each submit a model of leadership that includes roles and job descriptions. Discuss them together, pulling the strongest components from each.

Step 7 — Develop a formal proposal for church leadership

Once you have determined your channels of orphans ministry, the strategies you would like to implement, and the leadership structure, you will need to organize all of this into a formal proposal that can be presented to your church leadership for their approval and blessing.

When you first approach the staff members, elders, deacons, or the missions committee about your desire to begin an orphans ministry, be sure to communicate that you are seeking their approval, not their active involvement in yet another program.

Today's church leaders are already stretched thin as they lead and serve the local church; most simply do not have the time to undertake additional ministry programs. Many, however, will be receptive to others wanting to provide leadership to new initiatives such as an orphans ministry. Be sure to communicate your desire for their input and counsel as you move forward.

As you consider your presentation, keep in mind that you are primarily trying to accomplish two things:

1. **Cast the Vision**

   Many people are unfamiliar with what a church orphans ministry can look like and the tremendous impact it can make. For this reason, it is important to cast a vision for church orphans ministry by presenting stories of what other churches have done. You can use the DVD in this guide for that purpose or tell some of the stories that have been scattered through these pages. The probability is that at the beginning of the meeting, most in the room will envision a small ministry that will help a couple families to adopt. Your job is to make sure that by the end of the meeting they have a picture of how God has used orphans ministries all over the country to do some unbelievable and exciting things.

2. **Present the Plan**

   After you have cast the vision, the first question you can expect is "How are you going to do that?" Presenting a well-designed plan will help your leadership understand how and when you are going to carry out the various pieces of your team's vision.

At the very least, your plan should include:

    a. a brief summary of the process you have undergone thus far

    b. a description of your chosen channel(s) and the rationale for this choice

    c. your proposed strategies and the expected timing and resources for each

    d. your proposed leadership structure

    e. next steps

On-Board Tool 7 _____ Page 41

Sample Leadership Proposal

This tool provides you with an example of a proposal that could be presented to your church leaders.

Other Tools and Ideas_____

Prepare a document that summarizes the major Bible passages concerning orphans and adoption (see appendix A).

Provide a theological overview as a supplement to your proposal. (Visit www.HopeForOrphans.com and click on the "Church Orphans Ministry" button to find a sample of this and other helpful resources.)

Prepare a fact sheet with relevant statistics about the orphan crisis. It can be shocking for most to see the scope of the need. Two websites that will be helpful for these kinds of statistics are:

www.adoptuskids.org

    Includes national foster-care statistics.

www.unicef.org

    Look particularly in the publications section for reports on orphans worldwide. At the time of this writing, the most recent UNICEF report on estimated orphan numbers is *Children on the Brink 2004: A joint report of new orphans estimates and a framework for action.*

Step 8 — Launch your orphans ministry!

Once you have received approval from your church leadership, you can plan your launch. Most often this is done during a worship service. See On-Board Tool 8 for a list of ideas for a Launch Sunday. Of course, you can launch any time of year, but here are some key times that can be a good fit:

- Sanctity of Human Life Sunday—January, third Sunday

  You can employ use of the phrase "Pro-life ... for a lifetime" to indicate that you are not only looking out for the unborn but all children in our world who are vulnerable.

- National Foster-Care Month—May

- National Adoption Month—November

One of the most effective ways to engage your church at the time of the launch is to announce a church-wide project. For example, consider taking the month after your launch to sponsor a shoe or school-supply drive for orphans and waiting children. This will get everyone, including the children, involved. For a list of organizations that can help you host such a drive, see Appendix B.

Once you have launched the ministry, start with the first initiatives in your plan and begin growing in your understanding of orphans ministry. Most new initiatives start small. Remember that what God did in Brenham, Texas, (page 13) started with a simple support group. Learn what works. Learn what ministry resources are available and how to use them. Build on your successes. Become an expert in orphans ministry. If you see success in the first steps, you will then have the ability to grow and increase.

You will find that as you are faithful to take the first steps, opportunities to go deeper will come. One trip to an orphanage may turn into a long-term partnership with that orphanage. One small-group Bible study committed to providing a supportive environment for adoptive parents may expand into a well-established support group ministry. Your advocacy efforts for one child may result in that child plus dozens of fellow orphans being adopted through a hosting program in your church. You never know when your small step of faithfulness will be one that God turns into a giant leap for His kingdom.

Be deliberate about engaging the entire church, not just the orphans-ministry team. Be creative and open to new ideas coming from within your congregation. Spend time meeting with people in the community who are involved with orphans and waiting children. Some of your best ideas will come from these meetings. Stay in communication with other church orphans ministries in your city. Some of the most exciting things in the country are happening in the context of partnerships between churches. This includes one partnership of more than forty churches in one city! As you begin and sustain new initiatives, document how God is working and keep the people of your congregation updated. And remember always to give God the glory for how He is working.

As you've seen throughout these pages, there are a multitude of ways for your church to engage the needs of orphans and waiting children and, as Deuteronomy 24:19 describes, leave your sheaves behind. We trust the eight steps laid out in this guide have provided you with the blueprints for a dynamic orphans ministry in your church and that the tools to follow will help you launch it!

On-Board Tool 8 _____Page 46

Orphans Ministry Launch Ideas

This list will help you think through some possibilities for your launch Sunday.

Other Tools and Ideas_____

Hold a city-wide prayer vigil for waiting children in your foster-care system and see what God does in terms of partnership with other churches.

Assign a team archivist to collect photos of events and adoptive and foster families and assimilate them into a scrapbook that will help your team "remember His wonders which He has done" (Psalm 105:5a).

Eight On-Board Tools

to Help You *Get Started*

The enclosed DVD has been created to help you cast a vision to others in your church. Dennis Rainey, president of FamilyLife, will introduce you to a variety of people who have seen God move in their church in powerful ways on behalf of orphans.

As you read in Step 1 (page 6), approaching a key leader in your church and helping him or her understand your vision is a crucial part of establishing an orphans ministry. Because you may have a limited time to meet with this ministry leader, the DVD has been designed to be viewed in less than ten minutes. The DVD will cast the vision; your part will be to lay out how you would like to proceed and to ask your leader if he would be available to help you understand protocol and procedure along the way. Remember, you are not asking him to lead this ministry, nor are you presenting a comprehensive plan; you are simply asking for their blessing and their assistance as you move forward.

Take an evening to walk your group through the following prayer points. If you spend an average of ten minutes on each one, it will take about two hours to cover the entire list.

1. Pray through scriptures that address God's heart for the orphan (see Appendix A).

2. Praise God for how He has been working around the country and for what He is already doing in your church in this area.

3. Ask God to reveal what He wants to do through your church on behalf of the orphan.

4. Ask God if there are particular regions of the world He would have you focus on. Some find it helpful to have a world map available.

5. Pray that God would give both your congregation and your church leadership a growing passion to be used on behalf of the orphan.

6. Pray that God would assemble the right team at your church to accomplish His purposes.

7. Pray for the children whose lives God wants to change through your church. Consider printing out pictures and descriptions of children from Internet photo listings and praying for several children by name.

8. Pray that God would give you His creativity in coming up with ways to best care for orphans and waiting children.

9. Pray that God would show you how the orphans ministry might fit into existing programs in your church (missions, children's ministry, etc.).

10. Pray that God would provide divine appointments with:

- church leadership
- others in the congregation
- orphan-care organizations (see Appendix B)
- other church orphans ministries (see Appendix C)
- other Christians in your city who share your passion
- key people in local adoption agencies, foster-care offices, crisis pregnancy centers, etc.

11. Pray that God might bring revival to your church and other churches in your community through orphans ministry.

12. Pray that above all, God would be the one glorified through whatever He decides to do through your church.

To start off your brainstorming time as a team, dream together by responding to the following questions. Display the answers so that everyone can see them.

1. There are 143 million orphans in the world today. What would have to happen to ensure that *every one* of these children had regular contact with a follower of Christ?

2. If you had one million dollars to do the greatest good for the greatest number of orphans, what would you do? Similarly, what would you do with one thousand dollars?

3. If your church leadership said they were going to make orphans ministry their number one priority for the next year, what would you mobilize your church to do?

4. If you had the freedom to spend the next year doing anything you wanted full-time on behalf of the orphan, what would you do?

5. Now that you have been thinking outside of some of your normal boundaries, brainstorm all that your church could do to care for orphans.

One way to get a clearer picture of how God may have equipped your church for certain channels of orphans ministry is to look at your current situation. Filling in the chart below and answering the questions at the bottom of the page will help you assess areas of particular strength and will bring clarity to what channels you might consider pursuing.

	What resources do we currently have that could help in this channel?	**What experience do our people bring to the table in each channel?**
Orphan Care	Example: We have a missions department that sends out five short-term teams each year.	Example: Church members John and Ann Smith were missionaries in Guatemala for eight years and did a lot of work with orphans.
Adoption	Example: Our church has a strong relationship with a crisis pregnancy center.	Example: We have five adoptive families in our church.
Foster Care	Example: We have three sets of foster parents in our church.	Example: Church member Sara Green is a child welfare supervisor for the state.

What are the strengths of our church?

What is distinctive about our church's mission? (For example, some churches have a heavy emphasis on world missions while others emphasize the immediate community around them. These distinctions may be the difference between an orphan-care church and a foster-care church.)

Based simply on our current situation and on the time we have spent praying, which channels of orphans ministry seem to make the most sense for our church?

5

The following worksheets are designed to help you to identify your three-year objectives as well as your strategies to meet each of these objectives. The first three pages of this tool provide examples of how these worksheets can be used for each of the channels of church orphans ministry discussed in Step 4. The fourth page is for you to record your team's proposed objectives and strategies.

International and Private Domestic Adoption Channel - Example		
Current Situation Summary	• The Browns, Wilsons, and Washingtons have adopted seven children altogether internationally, domestically, and from foster care. They desire to share their varied experiences in order to encourage others. • There are currently several adoptive families in our church looking for support.	
	Objectives	**Strategies**
Year 1	We will provide a supportive environment for adoptive families and begin to establish a ministry that educates our congregation on the process of adoption.	• Establish a monthly support group for adoptive and foster families within our church and community • Hold one evening informational meeting about the process of adoption. Invite local adoption agencies and foster-care representatives to be in attendance.
Year 2	We will use our first year support group experiences to support our pastoral or biblical counseling staff in both pre- and post-adoptive lay counseling. We will establish a nucleus of ten committed families that will work to raise awareness and provide more formalized adoption education.	• Identify and/or develop materials that can be used by pastoral or biblical counseling staff in pre- and post-adoptive counseling. • Offer an all-day adoption education workshop for our congregation and other believers in the community.
Year 3	We will have established a mature ministry that mentors other churches in the areas of post-adoptive support and pre-adoptive education. We will work with other churches establish a local network of church adoption and orphan-care ministries.	• We will conduct a weekend workshop for other churches in our community on how to provide adoptive support and education • We will formalize a network of local church adoption and orphan-care ministries and provide ongoing support and encouragement for these ministries.

Orphan-Care Channel - Example		
Current Situation Summary	• Our church missions team has an existing church planting strategy in Uganda. • Our church's goal is to plant ten churches in the next ten years. • Bill and Carrie Logan are our church planting missionaries in Uganda and have seven years experience working with Ugandan orphans. • Our church body currently has a passion and vision for Uganda.	
	Objectives	**Strategies**
Year 1	We will have engaged our entire church body in meeting the needs of Ugandan orphans, built relationships with key organizations, and designed a comprehensive blueprint with the missions team for execution of our three year plan.	• Partner with orphan-care organization to host a drive to gather material goods for an existing Ugandan orphanage with the intent of increasing congregation's awareness of the needs of Ugandan orphans. • Establish a prayer bulletin board with pictures of Ugandan orphans • Identify key organizations that can help with development of children's homes (construction, administration, staffing, etc. ...) • Work with missions team to formulate blueprint for three year execution plan to build three children's homes.
Year 2	According to our plan, we will have planted one church with an attached children's home at the end of our second year.	• Identify which church plant is the best candidate for our first children's home • Work with partner organizations to construct home. • Organize two trips from church to decorate and supply children's home. • Identify house parents and additional part time staff need for home. • Work with partner organizations to establish administrative infrastructure for home.
Year 3	We will work within the church planting strategy of our missions team to establish a children's home (six-eight children and a set of house parents) as an integral part of each of our church plants in Uganda. Our goal is to have three new churches with attached children's homes at the end of three years.	• Repeat year two strategies along with two additional strategic church plants • Re-evaluate current situation and determine future steps to expand orphans-ministry strategy in Uganda.

Foster Care and Foster-Care Adoption Channel - Example	
Current Situation Summary	• The Taylors and Williams are currently foster parents. • The Simmons have adopted two children from foster care. • Each of these families has a desire to be a resource to the social workers in our local foster-care department and to equip others in the church to foster parent and adopt from foster care. • We have a well established prayer team in our church.

	Objectives	Strategies
Year 1	In partnership with our church prayer team, we will establish a prayer ministry for our local county social workers and the children in our state foster-care system.	• In partnership with local foster-care workers, assemble a comprehensive portfolio of waiting child profiles that can be used in a variety of ways in our prayer initiative. • During the Christmas season, take gifts to our county social workers to let them know we appreciate them. • Assign members of our team to be prayer partners with county workers. Prayer partners will call them workers monthly to ask for prayer requests.
Year 2	We will expand our prayer strategy and partner with the county office to establish ways to recruit foster and adoptive families.	• Establish a system for insuring that every waiting child in the portfolio is prayed for by someone on a daily basis, using the waiting child portfolio assembled in year one. • Host two informational meetings for those interested in foster parenting or adopting from foster care.
Year 3	We will mobilize believers in other churches to serve needs of our local foster-care offices so that their capacity to serve children is increased. We will also provide a consistent stream of foster and adoptive parents and will assist the county in executing the necessary training.	• Conduct a comprehensive survey among local foster-care offices to determine areas where skilled professionals in the church can leverage their abilities to support the ongoing work of local social workers. • Establish quarterly informational meetings at the church for recruiting foster and adoptive parents. Regularly invite other churches in community to attend.

Strategy Development Worksheet		
Current Situation Summary		
	Objectives	Strategies
Year 1		
Year 2		
Year 3		

Does your church currently have a prescribed leadership structure for new ministries? If so, what are its basic elements?

If it does not, what would you say are the most effective ministries currently operating in your church?

How are they structured?

What changes, if any, would need to be made to this structure to make it conducive to orphans ministry?

Do you have the people you need to fill your ideal structure? Who are possible candidates?

If you have no candidates for certain positions, you can (a) choose to change your leadership structure temporarily or (b) choose to wait and pray that God will bring the right people.

On-Board
Tool

7

Sample Leadership Proposal
*Step 7: Develop a formal proposal
for church leadership*

First Community Church (FCC)

Orphans Ministry Preliminary Overview

Introduction

In recent years certain members/deacons of FCC have developed personal convictions toward the needs of orphans and, desire to personally adopt a child or children into their home, Lord willing. As these individuals have become more knowledgeable of the needs, the convictions of these individuals have expanded to include the desire for churches, including FCC, to be actively involved in an orphans ministry.

These individuals have committed themselves to research the feasibility, resources available, and resources necessary for developing an orphans ministry at FCC. It is the hope of these individuals that this ministry will develop awareness, compassion, and conviction to minister to orphans as much as they would widows, the homeless, or any other needy group.

This overview seeks to generally describe the initial thoughts and objectives associated with this idea.

Objective

The primary objective is to minister to and meet the needs of orphans by developing an outreach through FCC. It is recommended that the ministry start small but include steps to accommodate an expanding vision. Following are three suggested phases with possible applications. It is also recommended that subsequent phases not be pursued until prior phases are well established. Further, the phases are expected to be cumulative, not transitional or substitutive.

Phase One: Awareness

Description

Develop awareness among church members of the existence and needs of orphans and God's call to minister to them. Ways to make church members aware include:

- bulletin board displays with orphan statistics, country information, and a description of needs. Information on particular orphanages in particular countries would be collected with a standard statistical and informational format to be rotated periodically (such as every 60 days)
- periodic bulletin panel or insert, FCC member news, and prayer needs
- sermons/teachings on orphans and God's perspective; perhaps an introductory sermon followed by a teaching class

Timing

This phase could begin within sixty days and would be expected to continue as a basic component of the ministry.

Resources

The first resource sought is simply the endorsement and support of the FCC elders to commit to pursuing the establishment of this orphans ministry.

It is anticipated that this phase of the ministry would require limited financial resources (no more than $500) and minimal commitment from two individuals. Bob and Jane Smith are prepared to be responsible for initiating and developing the ministry and garnering assistance from other interested members. It is anticipated that additional interested members will surface to assist in some of the administration and projects.

Phase Two: Outreach

Description

Develop practical and meaningful opportunities for members of FCC to personally and collectively minister to orphans. This phase could be broken into two components, domestic and international.

Domestic

- Possibly ally with a crisis pregnancy center.

International

- Partner with an FCC missionary or other reputable ministry for the purpose of FCC, as a church body, adopting one or more orphanages to minister to.

- Provide clothing, food, over-the-counter medicines, and hygiene supplies through coordinated donations.

- Solicit donations of these supplies from manufacturers and local suppliers/vendors.

- Investigate short-term ministry possibilities to deliver materials, conduct VBS, and work projects.

- Consider allying with local adoption agencies (no exclusive partnerships) for referrals.

Timing

This phase would begin in some form in six to twelve months from the beginning of the ministry.

Resources

The second phase of the ministry would require significantly more financial and human commitment, but is anticipated not to be required for six to twelve months. Furthermore, it is expected that the ministry funding would be analyzed and allocated through the normal budgeting processes.

Since it is difficult to estimate costs in this early stage, it is suggested that FCC allocate a prudent amount in the first year and manage the ministry within the budget, then re-assess the ministry opportunities in the second year.

With regard to human resources, it has been suggested that a care group, could embrace the orphans ministry much like they currently do for FCC missionaries. However, it is anticipated that the orphans ministry would require more involvement and greater hands-on responsibility.

Another option regarding human resources would be the formation of a ministry team much like that of the children's worship, etc.

Phase Three: Adoption

Description

It is anticipated that a natural outflow of Phases One and Two will be an increased desire among FCC families to adopt orphans into their homes. Consequently, once Phases One and Two are well established, it would be prudent to develop practical means to encourage, guide, and support FCC families who have developed a ministry conviction to adopt a child.

- Direct members to reputable sources for practical guidance.
- Uilize the experience of others to develop a guide to the process.
- Investigate the need for a Christian worldview-based support group of adoptive families.
- Leverage relationship with an orphanage or orphanages to facilitate and streamline the adoption process.
- Explore options for providing financial assistance through church budget, direct donations, and matching funds from foundations.
- Investigate the possibility of establishing a legal foundation dedicated to receiving donations for the purpose of providing financial assistance to adopting families.

It is also an objective of this initiative to explore opportunities to make the adoption process as economical, efficient, and inviting as possible.

It is not an objective of this ministry for FCC to act as its own adoption agency, or to directly advise infertile couples in the area of family planning or medical issues beyond normal counseling parameters.

Timing

Phase Three would be contingent upon the success of Phases One and Two. It is anticipated that Phase Three would require six to twelve months of development and would not be viable for implementation for at least eighteen months following the beginning of Phase One.

Resources

Effective administration of Phases One, Two, and Three will likely require at least a part-time staff person or dedicated volunteer and a considerably larger budget, which is difficult to estimate at this time. However, as previously mentioned, it is assumed that funds will be limited. Therefore, it is recommended that the ministry be managed within an available budget.

Strategy

The general strategy contemplated at this time is for FCC to leverage its existing contacts and relationships in certain countries for the purpose of establishing a direct alliance with and ministry to reputable orphanages. Through this direct alliance, it is anticipated that effective and efficient relationships and processes could be developed resulting in prudent and efficient ministry and potentially a less burdensome adoption process.

Outside Resources

Early inquiries of resources for this initiative have resulted in locating the following:

Bethlehem Baptist Church—Minneapolis, Minnesota

FamilyLife's Hope for Orphans—Little Rock, Arkansas

Brenham's First Baptist Church—Brenham, Texas

Shaohannah's Hope—McClean, Virginia

Next Steps:

1. Get endorsement from elders.

2. Gather statistics and information on specific countries, orphanages, and children.

3. Develop informational channels.

4. Target a specific orphanage and begin relationship development.

5. Engage couples interested in adoption.

6. Continue building relationships with outside resources.

Adapted from A Proposal for Orphans Ministry at the Bible Church of Little Rock *by Bryan Richardson and Phil Krause. Used by permission.*

The following is a list of ideas for components of your Launch Sunday:

Sermon

- Ask your pastor to deliver a sermon on the orphan.
- Show Dennis and Barbara Rainey's message *The Christian's Response to the Fatherless* available at www.HopeforOrphans.com.
- Identify someone on your team that would be permitted to give the sermon on the biblical mandate to care for the orphan.

Testimony

Consider including testimonies from:

- adoptive parents
- foster parents
- adopted children
- adult adoptees

Video

- Steven Curtis Chapman—*When Love Takes You In*
- Compile pictures of orphans, adoptive families, and foster families in your church. Build a visual presentation set to music. The song "He Knows My Name" works well.

Ceremony

Hold a mass dedication for all the children in your church who have been adopted.

Worship

- Ask your worship leader to select songs that emphasize our salvation and our adoption into God's family.
- Ask the children's choir to perform. If you have enough adopted children, ask them to sing.
- Ask adopted children to read scriptures on caring for the orphan.

Guests

Invite local adoption agencies, orphan-care organization, and crisis pregnancy centers to set up displays to give your congregation opportunities to get involved in various aspects of orphan care.

Displays

- Gather pictures of adoptive and foster families and create a display on a prominent church bulletin board.
- Print pictures and descriptions of waiting children from the Internet and create a prayer bulletin board.

Appendix A

A Scriptural Summary of the Orphan, the Fatherless, and Adoption

Orphan

Exodus 22:22-24
You shall not afflict any widow or orphan. If you afflict him at all, and if he does cry out to Me, I will surely hear his cry; and My anger will be kindled, and I will kill you with the sword, and your wives shall become widows and your children fatherless.

Deuteronomy 10:18
He executes justice for the orphan and the widow, and shows His love for the alien by giving him food and clothing.

Deuteronomy 14:29
The Levite, because he has no portion or inheritance among you, and the alien, the orphan and the widow who are in your town, shall come and eat and be satisfied, in order that the Lord your God may bless you in all the work of your hand which you do.

Deuteronomy 16:11
And you shall rejoice before the Lord your God, you and your son and your daughter and your male and female servants and the Levite who is in your town, and the stranger and the orphan and the widow who are in your midst, in the place where the Lord your God chooses to establish His name.

Deuteronomy 16:14
And you shall rejoice in your feast, you and your son and your daughter and your male and female servants and the Levite and the stranger and the orphan and widow who are in your towns.

Deuteronomy 24:17
You shall not pervert the justice due an alien or an orphan, nor take a widow's garment in pledge.

Deuteronomy 24:19

When you reap your harvest in your field and have forgotten a sheaf in the field, you shall not go back to get it; it shall be for the alien, for the orphan, and for the widow, in order that the Lord your God may bless you in all the work of your hands.

Deuteronomy 24:20

When you beat your olive tree, you shall not go over the boughs again; it shall be for the alien, for the orphan, and for the widow.

Deuteronomy 24:21

When you gather the grapes of your vineyard, you shall not go over it again; it shall be for the alien, for the orphan, and for the widow.

Deuteronomy 26:12

When you have finished paying all the tithe of your increase in the third year, the year of tithing, then you shall give it to the Levite, to the stranger, to the orphan and to the widow, that they may eat in your towns and be satisfied.

Deuteronomy 26:13

You shall say before the Lord your God, "I have removed the sacred portion from my house, and also have given it to the Levite and the alien, the orphan and the widow, according to all Your commandments which You have commanded me; I have not transgressed or forgotten any of Your commandments."

Deuteronomy 27:19

"Cursed is he who distorts the justice due an alien, orphan, and widow." And all the people shall say, "Amen."

Job 24:9

Others snatch the orphan from the breast, And against the poor they take a pledge.

Job 29:12

Because I delivered the poor who cried for help, And the orphan who had no helper.

Job 31:16-18

If I have kept the poor from their desire, Or have caused the eyes of the widow to fail, Or have eaten my morsel alone, And the orphan has not shared it (But from my youth he grew up with me as with a father, And from infancy I guided her),

Job 31:21-22

If I have lifted up my hand against the orphan, Because I saw I had support in the gate, Let my shoulder fall from the socket, And my arm be broken off at the elbow.

Psalm 10:14

You have seen it, for You have beheld mischief and vexation to take it into Your hand. The unfortunate commits himself to You; You have been the helper of the orphan.

Psalm 10:17-18
O Lord, You have heard the desire of the
*   humble;*
You will strengthen their heart, You will
*   incline Your ear*
To vindicate the orphan and the
*   oppressed,*
So that man who is of the earth will no
*   longer cause terror.*

Isaiah 1:17
Learn to do good;
Seek justice,
Reprove the ruthless,
Defend the orphan,
Plead for the widow.

Isaiah 1:23
Your rulers are rebels
And companions of thieves;
Everyone loves a bribe
And chases after rewards.
They do not defend the orphan,
Nor does the widow's plea come before
*   them.*

Jeremiah 5:28
"They are fat, they are sleek,
They also excel in deeds of wickedness;
They do not plead the cause,
The cause of the orphan, that they may
*   prosper;*
And they do not defend the rights of the
*   poor."*

Jeremiah 7:5-7
For if you truly amend your ways and
your deeds, if you truly practice justice
between a man and his neighbor, if you
do not oppress the alien, the orphan, or
the widow, and do not shed innocent
blood in this place, nor walk after other
gods to you own ruin, then I will let you
dwell in this place, in the land that I
gave to your fathers forever and ever.

Jeremiah 22:3
Thus says the Lord, "Do justice and
righteousness, and deliver the one who
has been robbed from the power of his
oppressor. Also do not mistreat or do
violence to the stranger, the orphan, or
the widow; and do not shed innocent
blood in this place."

Hosea 14:3
Assyria will not save us,
We will not ride on horses;
Nor will we say again, "Our god,"
To the work of our hands;
For in You the orphan finds mercy.

Zechariah 7:10
And do not oppress the widow or the
orphan, the stranger or the poor; and do
not devise evil in your hearts against one
another.

Malachi 3:5

"Then I will draw near to you for judgment; and I will be a swift witness against the sorcerers and against the adulterers and against those who swear falsely, and against those who oppress the wage earner in his wages, the widow and the orphan, and those who turn aside the alien and do not fear Me," says the Lord of hosts.

Orphans

Job 6:27

*You would even cast lots for the orphans
And barter over your friend.*

Job 22:9

*You have sent widows away empty,
And the strength of the orphans has been
    crushed.*

Job 24:3

*They drive away the donkeys of the
    orphans;
They take the widow's ox for a pledge.*

Psalm 94:6

*They slay the widow and the stranger
And murder the orphans.*

Isaiah 9:17

*Therefore the Lord does not take pleasure
    in their young men,
Nor does He have pity on their orphans
    or their widows;
For every one of them is godless and an
    evildoer,
And every mouth is speaking foolishness.
In spite of all this, His anger does not
    turn away
And His hand is still stretched out.*

Isaiah 10:2

*So as to deprive the needy of justice
And rob the poor of My people of their
    rights,
So that widows may be their spoil
And that they may plunder the orphans.*

Jeremiah 49:11

*Leave your orphans behind, I will keep
    them alive;
And let your widows trust in Me.*

Lamentations 5:3

*We have become orphans without a
    father,
Our mothers are like widows.*

John 14:18

*I will not leave you as orphans; I will
    come to you.*

James 1:27
Pure and undefiled religion in the sight of our God and Father is this: to visit orphans and widows in their distress, and to keep oneself unstained by the world.

Fatherless

Exodus 22:24
and My anger will be kindled, and I will kill you with the sword, and your wives shall become widows and your children fatherless.

Psalm 68:5
A father of the fatherless and a judge for the widows,
Is God in His holy habitation.

Psalm 82:3
Vindicate the weak and fatherless;
Do justice to the afflicted and destitute.

Psalm 109:9
Let his children be fatherless
And his wife a widow.

Psalm 109:12
Let there be none to extend lovingkindness to him,
Nor any to be gracious to his fatherless children.

Psalm 146:9
The Lord protects the strangers;
He supports the fatherless and the widow,
But He thwarts the way of the wicked.

Proverbs 23:10-11
Do not move the ancient boundary
Or go into the fields of the fatherless,
For their Redeemer is strong;
He will plead their case against you.

Ezekiel 22:7
They have treated father and mother lightly within you. The alien they have oppressed in your midst; the fatherless and the widow they have wronged in you.

Adoption

Romans 8:15
For you have not received a spirit of slavery leading to fear again, but you have received a spirit of adoption as sons by which we cry out, "Abba! Father!"

Romans 8:23

And not only this, but also we ourselves, having the first fruits of the Spirit, even we ourselves groan within ourselves, waiting eagerly for our adoption as sons, the redemption of our body.

Romans 9:4
who are Israelites, to whom belongs the adoption as sons, and the glory and the covenants and the giving of the Law and the temple service and the promises

Galatians 4:5
*so that He might redeem those who were
under the Law, that we might receive the
adoption as sons.*

Ephesians 1:5
*He predestined us to adoption as sons through
Jesus Christ to Himself, according to the kind
intention of His will*

Instances of Orphans in Scripture

Lot in Genesis 11:27-28
The Daughters of Zelophehad in Numbers
    27:1-5
Jotham in Judges 9:16-21
Mephibosheth in 2 Samuel 9:3
Joash in 2 Kings 11:1-12
Esther in Esther 2:7

Instances of "Adoption"

Moses "adopted" by Pharaoh's daughter
    Exodus 2:1-10
Job cared for unnamed orphans
    Job 31:16-18
Mordecai "adopted" Esther
    Esther 2:7
Jesus "adopted" by Joseph
    Matthew 1:18-24
Every Christian has been adopted by God
    through Jesus Christ
    Ephesians 1:5

Appendix **B**

Key Organizations That Can Help You Implement Orphans-Ministry Strategies

Buckner International Orphan Care

Contact: www.helporphans.org

Areas of Focus: Afghanistan, Belize, Belarus, Bulgaria, China, Croatia, Columbia, Cuba, Ecuador, Ethiopia, Egypt, Guyana, Guatemala, Haiti, Honduras, India, Israel, Kazakhstan, Kenya, Kosovo, Latvia, Mexico, Moldova, Nigeria, Peru, Philippines, Romania, Russia, United States, Uganda, Ukraine and Zambia.

How they can help your church: mission trips, gifts for orphans and orphanages, organization of drives for shoes and other resources, hosting programs

Children's HopeChest

Contact: www.hopechest.org

Areas of Focus: Romania, Russia, Ukraine

How they can help your church: orphanage sponsorship, mission trips

Children's Hope International

Contact: www.chifoundation.org

Areas of Focus: China, Guatemala, India, Russia, Vietnam, Kazakhstan, Columbia, United States

How they can help your church: hosting program, medical assistance, gifts for orphanages

GAIN—Global Aid Network

Contact: www.gainusa.org

Areas of Focus: Ukraine, Belarus, Russia, Cambodia, Moldova, Tajikistan, Uganda

How they can help your church: mission trips, care pack drives (school supplies), orphanage sponsorship

Life International

Contact: www.lifeintl.org

Areas of Focus: helping churches establish their own adoption funding program

How they can help your church: provide the set-up and administration of an adoption fund in your church's name at no cost to you

Shaohannah's Hope

Contact: www.shaohannahshope.org

Areas of Focus: helping churches establish their own adoption funding program

How they can help your church: helpful resources for initiating orphans ministry in your church and for starting an adoption fund. Their Building Bridges piece on church orphans ministry includes a DVD of the Steven Curtis Chapman music video, *When Love Takes You In*, which is excellent for casting vision to church leadership, your congregation, and others at adoption education events.

Vision Trust

Contact: OrphanCare@VisionTrust.org

Areas of Focus: Brazil, Central African Republic, Dominican Republic, India, Peru, Myanmar, Thailand

How they can help your church: starting orphan-care ministry in your church, child sponsorship, mission trips

World Orphans

Contact: www.worldorphans.com

Areas of Focus: worldwide

How they can help your church: with your church's underwriting, they can build church-based orphans homes around the world for $4-8,000 each.

FamilyLife's Hope for Orphans continues to add new organizations that can be a resource to your church. For the most up-to-date list and other helpful resources, visit www.HopeforOrphans.com and click on the "Church Orphans Ministry" button.

Church Name	Ministry Name	City, ST	Website
Bethlehem Baptist Church	MICAH Fund	Minneapolis, MN	www.micahfund.org
Brenham's First Baptist Church	Forever Families and Here I Am Ministries	Brenham, TX	www.foreverfamilies.org www.orphanministries.com
Christ Chapel Bible Church	x	Fort Worth, TX	http://www.ccbcfamily.org /orphan_care/index.html
Colorado Community Church	Project 1.27	Aurora, CO	www.project127.com
Healing Place Church	His Heart for Orphans	Baton Rouge, LA	www.healingplacechurch.org
Irving Bible Church	Tapestry	Irving, TX	http://tapestry.irvingbible.org
Southeast Christian Church	Southeast Christian Adoption & Orphan Care Ministry	Louisville, KY	www.southeastchristian.org

Contact Person	Contact Info	Ministry Focus
Maridel Sandberg	maridel@micahfund.org	financial assistance
Jay & Suzanne Faske Robert & Kamala Kitzman	faskefamily@hughes.net robertkk@sbcglobal.net	adoption education, adoption support group, orphan care, medical missions
Scott & Monica Brown	orphancare@christchapelbc.org	adoption, orphan care, support for birth, foster and adoptive families
Lisel Harkless	info@project127.com	foster-care adoption
Tommy and Aimeé Poché	ephesians1five@cox.net	adoption workshops, adoption support group, adoption/orphan e-newsletter, orphan care
Michael and Amy Monroe	tapestry@irvingbible.org	adoption and foster-care support and education; orphan care
Kent Hatfield	kent.hatfield@skofirm.com	adoption, orphan care